P9-DHA-456

ARTIST AND ADVOCATE AN ESSAY ON CORPORATE PATRONAGE

B 74: 007

Library of Congress Catalog Card Number 67-24916
Copyright © 1967 by Renaissance Editions, Inc.
No part of this book may be reproduced in any form
without permission in writing from the publisher.
Manufactured in the United States of America

TABLE OF CONTENTS

THE
NEW
COLLECTORS

by Nina Kaiden

In the first quarter of this century, William Randolph Hearst brought the passion for wholesale collecting to its most exquisite refinement. He would buy in gross quantities such things as 16th century Norman chateaux, which were torn from their foundations, numbered stone by stone for do-it-yourself reassembly, and then abandoned in fusty warehouses along with cases of armor, broadswords and pewter mugs. Such indulgence of indiscriminate thing-hunger died with the income tax and the depression, which tended to discourage simple magpie acquisitiveness, and the drive toward the accumulation of First Dynasty mummies and early Christian catacombs died away in this country.

True, there are still men like Norton Simon who are willing and able to contend with The National Gallery for a $5 million Leonardo. But there aren't many private collectors like Simon. To take the place of the great accumulators of the past, another kind of collector has risen.

These new collectors are the corporations. Collecting by business institutions is not entirely new, but it has changed dramatically. In its early days the practice was limited to displaying time-honored reproductions and corporate heirlooms like an original Coleman's Mustard poster, framed bills of lading in Spencerian script, portraits of gimlet-eyed founding fathers—perhaps even a company's first left-hand screw that for three generations controlled pressure in the building's steam boilers.

Today's corporate collectors are as different from yesterday's as they can be. Almost without exception their interest extends beyond the safe and the accepted. This is not to say that they object to the old because it is old, or buy the new for the sake of its newness. Chase Manhattan, Seagram's and others own many traditional works of art and antiques, but the main thrust of collecting interest is toward the imaginative efforts by the most avant garde artists who are finding new ways of saying old things, using new techniques, materials and forms. The corporate collector is likely to be open and responsive to innovation, no less so in his business decisions than in his feel for the contemporary world of art.

If one could score executives on the basis of their support of new ideas, new concepts, unique solutions to business problems, the ones with the highest marks would probably also be the ones most ready to accept and comprehend the fresh ideas of today's painters and sculptors.

Perhaps this is indicative of the trend toward more youthful management and its pervasive influence in the current corporate

Lee Boltin

Chase Manhattan Bank, New York City
Alexander Calder, *untitled mobile*

structure. These men are part of that new breed of executives for whom yesterday belongs to the archeologists and today becomes history almost as soon as they board the 5:19 for Greenwich. They act on the basis of an unerring instinct for excellence—in a line of advertising copy, in the shape of a new bathtub faucet, or in the forms and colors of a Motherwell abstract.

What emerges from many conversations with corporate collectors who have sought help and advice over the years is that in most instances a company begins collecting because someone high enough on the table of organization is personally persuaded that an aesthetic environment is vital to the dynamics of the company. He is able to muster enough sound arguments to win his peers over to the idea. Richard J. Whalen, writing elsewhere in this volume, calls this man the "advocate," and describes Arthur Harris' role as the advocate of art at The Mead Corporation. Not infrequently, the advocate is the corporation's chief officer, as in the case of International Business Machines, where Thomas J. Watson, president, started the company collecting works of art from each of the seventy-nine countries where it was doing business. Now IBM has its own 57th Street art gallery where it presents exhibitions throughout the year.

Ezra Stoller

American Republic Insurance Company, Des Moines, Iowa
Alexander Calder, *"Spunk of the Monk"* stabile

The advocate of art at Philip Morris, Inc., is George Weissman, president, who was responsible for that company's travelling exhibition called "Pop and Op." It was the first major national exhibition of graphics reflecting these trends. Many of the works were commissioned by the company, which encouraged the artists to the widest experimentation. Among the results were examples of Pop art that used such contemporary materials as silver foil, metallic plastic, styrene and vinyl. The sixty-five works in the collection also included examples of Op art chosen from American and European portfolios. Both art trends represented were still highly controversial, but the corporation saw in them cultural expressions that merited exposure and left the question—"is it art?"—to the viewer. The exhibition is currently in its second year, touring communities as diverse as New York City and Columbus, Georgia. Simultaneously the Pop works were sent abroad in cooperation with the U. S. Information Service, to seventeen countries in Europe, Asia and Latin America.

Another activist was the late Walter Paepcke, who started Container Corporation buying art for that company's institutional advertising campaign. He has his counterpart in almost every company that has won for itself the distinction of owning an im-

David Vestal

Philip Morris Incorporated, New York City
Sam Francis, *"Abstraction"*

portant collection of fine art.

The decision to spend corporate funds on works of art is not one that is taken lightly. It is usually preceded by a long and serious debate which recurs whenever a corporation considers support of the arts. The debate revolves around this central question: Does a corporation have the right to spend the stockholders' money on cultural projects that cannot clearly be shown to have a direct impact on the building of assets and the earning of profits?

More and more corporations are answering this question in the affirmative. Often their arguments take on a deep philosophical tone, and the reasoning that is coming more and more to be accepted is based on some ancient truths. The main thesis is that a corporation does not exist in a vacuum, but grows and prospers in direct relation to the growth and prosperity of the society in which it operates. Dr. Frank Stanton, president of CBS, recently declared:

"I am not sure that the arts are not ultimately the meeting ground where liberal education and progressive business come together. The purpose of liberal education is, basically, to enable us to make distinctions. The essence of successful business practice is to operate on distinctions. The arts carry distinctions to their logical, and very often their illogical, extremes. And so the first place to worry about American life losing its vital qualities or individualism is in the arts. If this happens, no liberal education will save our kind of society, and no business enterprise will long prosper in what is left to it."

This kind of thinking is shared by many of the new breed of executives, and their number is growing steadily. There are, however, more immediate and direct advantages for the corporate collector than helping to shape his long-range environment. Management executives have come to recognize the many practical benefits in public relations terms—among them, building goodwill and establishing a reputation for progressiveness.

This reputation is vital to the modern business institution. It influences consumer acceptance of its products; helps attract dynamic young talents to the executive roster; satisfies stockholder interest in its ability to compete; and contributes significantly to heightened respect from all segments of society.

Standard Oil of New Jersey has been a pioneer not only in the support of the arts, but also in establishing the precedents for such uses of corporate funds. Through a friendly lawsuit by a shareholder in another New Jersey company, a clear legal right was established for a corporation to support educational institutions that bore no direct relationship to the specific field of the corporation. Standard Oil began exercising this right some fifteen years ago in developing art programs serving the Western Hemisphere. In cooperation with the Pan American Union, it most recently presented in Washington an exhibition of works by young Latin American artists, which had been chosen through contests in each country.

In some instances modern art forms are translated into such practical applications as the architecture of a new plant or headquarters, interior design, corporate symbol or advertising programs. One of the most venturesome companies is Joseph E. Seagram & Sons, Inc., whose building on Park Avenue is itself a work of art. That outstanding bronze and glass shaft was designed by Mies van der Rohe, and it is now embellished with some 500 works of art and antiques. Three blocks away stands another distinguished structure—the CBS Building designed by the late Eero Saarinen. In a sense, CBS is the prototype for the enlightened corporation: architecture, interior design, art collection, corporate symbol—all represent some of the finest artistic expressions of our time.

Reynolds Metals Company sponsors an architectural competi-

Robert Damora

Columbia Broadcasting System, Inc., New York City
Center, Henry Moore, "*Locking Piece*" sculpture   Right, Franz Kline, "*Crosstown*"

tion in honor of Richard S. Reynolds, Sr., which carries a $25,000 award. The company also commissions sculptures in aluminum which are awarded as symbols to prize winners. Among the sculptors who have created such symbols are Seymour Lipton, Harry Bertoia, Leonard Baskin, and William Zorach.

However, to large segments of the public the most meaningful expression of corporate commitment probably lies in the sponsorship of contemporary art programs. Over the past ten years, corporations have become increasingly involved in the purchase of art and in the subsequent exposure of that art either in their own buildings or through travelling exhibitions.

In 1963, Clairol assembled a collection of fifty paintings, drawings, sculptures and prints on the theme of "Mother and Child" for an exhibition that was to tour for several years. The theme was a natural parallel to the company's "Does she or doesn't she?" mother-and-child advertising campaign, but the exhibition was kept free of commercial overtones. Some of the major works shown were borrowed, and a number of commissions were executed by contemporary artists. Once the artists allowed themselves to be reassured that they were not expected to do mothers and children with the same hair color, they produced some delightful treatments of the theme.

The S. C. Johnson Collection, assembled at a cost of $750,000, has been on the road in Europe, Asia and South America since 1961. When its travels are ended, the collection will go to the National Collection of the Arts at the Smithsonian Institution. All the works in the Johnson group are by American artists, starting with the romantic realism of Edward Hopper and Raphael Soyer, and going through the various changes in style and taste to the works of such contemporary artists as Larry Rivers and Robert Rauschenberg.

Another corporation using art to achieve an objective is the Singer Company, which built an art collection that would broaden its reputation beyond sewing machines to embrace its activity in electronics, business machines and infra-red reconnaissance techniques. Singer assembled a collection of contemporary paintings and sculptures which are displayed in its offices and principal showrooms throughout the country.

New York City abounds with office buildings which house corporate-sponsored art galleries and collections. American Greetings, Union Carbide, and Time, Inc., among others, regularly assemble museum-quality exhibitions which are open to the public. The story of art collecting by New York's big commercial banks—Chase Manhattan and Manufacturer's Hanover Trust, most notably—has been told and retold. On the West Coast, Lytton Savings & Loan maintains an art gallery with a full-time staff, the inspiration of Bart Lytton. And in Des Moines, Iowa, Watson Powell, president of the American Republic Insurance Company, has assembled one of the most exciting collections of contemporary American art for display in his company's building. It is worth the trip to Des Moines.

The list of corporate collectors seems endless. And, indeed, it has grown spectacularly in the decade and a half since Mead's program was initiated. But it still represents only a tiny handful of the thousands of corporations doing business in the U. S. today.

These companies also have a unique opportunity to bring art into the everyday experience of the American public. Even beyond this, however, is the chance to join with the pioneer collectors in realizing the potential of the new relationship between art and business. For the corporate collectors have been catalysts for the slow but sure start of a dialogue between business and the arts, a dialogue with major implications for our society. So far, business has been more of a listener than an active participant. Yes, cor-

Ezra Stoller

American Republic Insurance Company, Des Moines, Iowa
l. to r., Stephen Greene, *"The Family"*   Ludwig Sander, *untitled*
Bernard Langlais, *"Portrait of a Cow"*   Grace Hartigan, *"Since Rousseau"*   *19*

porations have purchased art and given it broader exposure than it might otherwise have had; some, through commissions, have even brought works of art into being that might not otherwise have existed. Though this will undoubtedly continue to be the bread-and-butter staple, it is not enough. The world of today calls for a closer relationship between business and the arts.

Because they are already conditioned to accept new ideas, the cultural innovators of today have a special responsibility to find new ways to explore the world of the arts. Perhaps one day there will be art cooperatives formed by corporations and joined with artists to sponsor projects too big for anyone to handle alone. Or corporations may create new museums. Or artists-in-residence may become corporate consultants.

After all, who would have thought that Chase and IBM would need art curators?

ART AT WORK IN ITS ENVIRONMENT

by Bartlett Hayes

At the beginning of this century there was, in Italy, an inquiring group of thinkers called Futurists among whom was a painter, Gino Severini. His long lifetime was crowded with change and he defined art by observing change. In his youth, Utopian ideals appeared to have been achieved at long last, or so it was assumed by political and economic leaders of the day. Their over-confidence vanished when the world plunged into its first global war. The Futurists, however, had recognized the signals of change, as artists so often prophetically do, and Severini described art as "the alteration of nature according to one's sensibility."

Two words determine the balanced wisdom of his point of view: one is *alteration* (the amount, or extent of it), the other is *sensibility* (the quality, or weight of it). Nature is the fulcrum; art is the relative and delicate balance itself. Note, moreover, that sensibility possesses a dual meaning: it is both rational and sensory. Alteration, on the other hand, is infinite in degree, ranging from the most finite description or characterization, to the most abstract symbol.

Let me examine the Severini viewpoint, that the alteration of nature and the sensibility with which it is accomplished is the essence of art. There is small reason to doubt that the alteration of nature is the pride of the modern scientific age and that the sensibility with which the alteration has been achieved by industry varies as much as it does in the case of art. Are the human insights behind modern science and engineering wholly different from those human insights which inspire the artist? Is not the alteration of nature a process common to both art and science?

Throughout the long centuries of recorded history, we can see how man has artistically altered his vision of his natural world; we also possess evidence of ways in which he has altered its physical character. He has furrowed the field for the seed and the harvest and broken the mountain to smelt the strength from it; he has piled stone upon stone to shelter his living and built temples to foster his spiritual being (paradoxically he fashions these with pomp and elegance; the paradox itself is art). He has hurdled the valleys and tunneled the hills, channeled the harbors and dammed up the rivers, leveled the forests, constructed the cities and plotted the highways that course their ways to them endlessly onward, building, renewing and building always. Thus the power of industry changes things, reshaping and altering nature.

But how sensitive is the control of these impetuous, compulsive, relentless operations? America has earned for itself the epithet materialistic, perhaps because elsewhere in the world, despite comparable physical growth, are still to be seen houses and monuments inherited from earlier generations. America owns little of such physical historical evidence. Forms have been borrowed eclectically, willfully destroyed and replaced. Accordingly, when a parallel is sought between the sensibility of art and the sensibility of industry, it is harder to find than the obvious parallel of alteration. The clutter of roadside commerce obscures all else. Nevertheless, an environment of sensibility may be found by seeking it.

Not long ago I walked into a tidy new Southwestern high school, spacious and attractively furnished, almost to the point of extravagance. I caught myself thinking, "All this for a school?" I knew better and learned better. The appearance of the old school had been dingy, I was told. Walls and floors had been monotonous. The pupils' behavior had been noisy and their discipline poor. In the new building, the atmosphere was pleasant and the student attitude was respectful, almost to the point of pride. Discipline was no longer a problem. The work for the teachers was thereby lightened and their relief resulted in a friendly student-teacher interchange which had been virtually absent before.

This interchange, in turn, resulted in better work. A utility closet had been remodeled into a small picture gallery because neither the school committee nor the architect had thought so far as to include one in the original specifications. Art was at work in the environment.

A few years ago a city bank moved across the street into a new location. The Renaissance facade of the old building had been constructed of heavy and dark-gray stone. The gloomy interior of the building had been lighted artificially by elaborate bronze fixtures. The walls were paneled in dark-stained oak. But the glass facade of the new building identified the exterior with the interior. The eye of the beholder was welcomed by the interior space, by the plants which now had light enough to grow, by the trimness of the fittings and by the sculpture which served not only to excite the eye, but also as a dividing wall. I wondered what effect this new environment might have on the bank's business. Upon investigating, I was informed by an administrative source that within the first six months of occupancy, the bank's several activities, including new accounts, had risen from 15 percent to 30 percent. Art was at work in the environment.

During World War II a serious problem of fatigue had developed in a parachute factory. It was necessary to concentrate at close distance on fine, strong stitching. The tension was such that if, during mid-afternoon, a thread broke on the machine, the alert young woman, whose temperament normally suited the task, would collapse in tears. Music had been introduced to alleviate tension, lights had been brightened to alleviate eyestrain and consequent nervous pressure, but their effect was minimal. Longer and more frequent rest periods were prescribed and scheduled, but even these provided slight relief. There remained, within the bleakness of the rest room, an anxiety to return to work because increased production meant increased pay. Moreover, the blank walls of the rest area were punctuated by windows that looked out against the equally confining bare, brick walls of the adjacent factory buildings. Everything was closeted. There was constantly a sense of that demanding, dominating machine close by.

Ultimately, on a hunch, some paintings were borrowed from a museum in the vicinity. The paintings were landscapes, for the most part, selected for differences in depth of focus and differences in geography and seasons of the year. Each week during the period of experiment, the half dozen pictures were exchanged for new ones. At the end of the fourth week, the paintings were collected, but as a test, no new ones replaced them. "Where are the paintings?" were the lamenting questions. "Aren't we going to have any more?" Work became erratic once again, so much so that it was necessary to announce that more paintings would be forthcoming the following weeks. Shortly thereafter, during the course of several random interviews, the charwoman who tended the rest area was asked if she had any opinion of the paintings. "Waal," went her considered reply, "before them pictures were here, they mostly talked about the girls who wasn't in the room; now they mostly talk about the pictures." Art was at work in the environment.

It is a fallacy to assume that art cannot have a function, or that its environmental presence cannot influence whoever comes within range. The problem, then, is how to develop an environment which will accomplish the sensitive, psychological responses which comprise the Good Society. One solution is, of course, to make more of it; but this poses a second problem, namely, how to demonstrate to the many leaders of the current society that the problem actually exists. Lacking a visible physical aesthetic heritage (to which I have already alluded), a large majority of the American people have managed to do pretty well achieving physical comforts without the refreshing nourishment which the several arts provide. The arts are thought of, therefore, as a sweet to follow the basic course. But this causes cultural malnutrition. Instead, might not the arts be savored as a staple ingredient, rich in cultural vitamins?

Nevertheless, it is important to move from situations as they are to others which can be judged as being potentially more desirable. This is the lesson which scientist and engineer have so beautifully articulated in evolving the social pattern which we call *today*. On the other hand, one may question whether people today are truly happier than people of yesterday; and what of the generation to come? Or, to phrase the question differently, is there something which our interlocking economy has failed to provide in order to justify its operations in behalf of social betterment?

I have already proffered an answer before posing the question: to increase the sensibility by which technology is advanced is to ally it to the function of art; to discover that art possesses a social function is to construct a bond between these two particles of society which may, by the grace of nature, produce a more stable behavioral compound than presently exists. In other words, the justification of the corporate world is the physical improvement of mankind; but, if man himself cannot be improved socially, emotionally, intellectually, intuitively and spiritually, is his physical enhancement really worth the effort?

The other essays in this volume document certain programs which identify a far-sighted awareness of the necessary partnership between the arts and humanities on the one hand, and the social or behavioral activities of the corporation on the other hand. Such partnership is truly *necessary*, for it promises a happier, more fruitful and more humane evolution of man than we have known heretofore. This may be an idealistic view, but ideals (to paraphrase the philosopher Francis Bacon) also serve for delight.

Webster suggests that to "call to" (ad-vocare) once had the meaning of calling for aid on the part of the caller, the supplicant. However, it was soon used to denote the one who supplies aid, or argues in behalf of the supplicant. This difference, this shift in meaning, is central to the theme, *Artist and Advocate*.

If modern industry can implement its own physical progress and, simultaneously, ensure the financial survival of those artistic enterprises and institutions which nourish the imaginative personnel who conduct the corporate operation, then one function of art is clear. It is indeed to extend the sensibility by which nature may be altered—a task close to the heart of executive enlightenment and essential throughout the corporate structure. In practical terms, to engage in this task means not only to be concerned for the artist himself, but also for the broad, cultural life of the community which the corporation shares. If the corporation is to perform wisely in its advocacy of the arts, it must understand throughout every level that it is also the supplicant in the original sense of *ad vocare* and must thereby call the artist to its own aid. For it is the artist who can make the alterations of the common environment all the more sensible.

ARTIST
AND
ADVOCATE

by Richard J. Whalen

The American businessman . . . must now come to terms with the artist. Artistic perception is as necessary to the modern manufacturer of consumer goods as engineering skill.

John Kenneth Galbraith

As responsible citizens of the Affluent Society, scores of U. S. corporations have heeded Galbraith's admonition in recent years, at least to the extent of acquiring and displaying fine art. The survey on the preceding pages, briefly describing a number of corporate collections, attests the maturity and social consciousness of the contemporary American business community. Yet the pride of businessmen in their involvement in art should be tempered by the realization that their role thus far has been generally passive. Corporations are conspicuously consuming culture, but relatively few of them are directly encouraging the artists, which, as Galbraith suggests, is what businessmen should be doing as a matter of enlightened self-interest. As corporate patronage matures, going beyond acquisition and display, businessmen and artists will be drawn into a continuing, mutually rewarding involvement, which will signal the full emergence of the corporation as a creative cultural force.

Obviously, the present stage of corporate patronage reflects the expanding cultural awareness of our society as a whole. Almost invariably, a corporation begins collecting because an influential individual within the executive hierarchy, who has a deep personal interest in art, urges such involvement. In the beginning, an advocate is indispensable, for every new idea in the business world must assert its claims against the established ideas and organized procedures that resist disruptive innovation. Moreover, because art lacks the obvious relevance to the corporation's interests of, say, a fresh marketing proposal, the advocate must lead the way in establishing a new frame of reference in which art is clearly relevant.

All too frequently, this unfamiliar exercise is stinted, with the result that corporate patronage gets stuck in the first stage of development. In deference to the influential advocate, art is "accepted" by the corporation, and justified by recourse to the elastic vocabulary of public relations. The soaring public prestige of art makes it a highly attractive corporate status symbol and image-builder. Such easy and plausible rationalization often gets art hung on the walls of the executive suite, but it doesn't win an enduring place for art *within* the corporate structure. The corporation is not so much patronizing art as it is subsidizing, temporarily, an executive pastime.

If this seductive deadend is to be avoided, the advocate must be determined to see his personal commitment to art transferred to the organization, which, of course, means relinquishing at least some of the control he exercised when the idea was entirely his. However, the offsetting gain is that support for art wins staff, budget, and, most important, *internal* prestige as a permanent corporate interest. It takes time and intellectual effort to see art as something more than a corporate status symbol, and to explore its meaning to a particular company and an entire society. The process often stirs passionate debate and even table-pounding disagreement. Men accustomed to deciding on plant locations and product mixes on the basis of hard, objective data must grope for intangibles and for a vocabulary to express their judgments. But growing up to new responsibility, and seizing new advantages, often involves painful adjustment.

If the experience of The Mead Corporation is any guide, the outcome of the intramural soul-searching can offer abundant and sometimes unexpected compensations. One of the nation's largest manufacturers of fine papers, paperboard, packaging and containers, Mead has developed, by deliberate stages extending over a decade, perhaps the most comprehensive program of art-support in American business. Its outlays for art are by no means the largest, nor is its collection the most distinguished, but it has come into contact with more than ten thousand artists in the course of its patronage. Throughout the country, Mead's deep and generous commitment has won the respect of those engaged in the creation of art; and the company is extending its patronage to the contemporary artists of Europe.

As in any sound and balanced relationship, benefits flow both ways, and Mead rightly offers no apology for the self-interest that goes hand in hand with its declared social responsibility. As a statement of the company philosophy declares: "The artist is the natural partner of the paper and packaging industry, for it is the artist's creativity, imagination and resourcefulness which gives life to the very materials Mead produces. The artist's work is an integral part of business life, and it is for this reason among others that Mead hopes to further creativity in this country by improving the forum for the American artist and his various audiences." The experience of Mead is worth considering in some detail for what it illustrates about achieving the alliance between businessman and artist that holds so much promise for both.

In Mead's case, the advocate of corporate involvement was an outsider when he took the plunge. Arthur L. Harris, president of his family's Atlanta Paper Company, decided in 1954 that his company's Christmas gift-giving policy was unsatisfactory. Casting about for an idea, he finally hit upon one that grew out of his personal interest in art as a local patron and small collector. He commissioned an original oil painting by George Beattie, an Atlanta artist, which was lithographed and distributed at Christmas. Among the few hundred recipients, Beattie's "Georgia Nocturne," an evocative nighttime impression of the state's famous Stone Mountain, produced responses ranging from delight to puzzlement. Harris had formerly sent customers a gift of paper-shell pecans. "Some people wrote back that they liked the picture," he recalls, "but where the hell were the pecans."

The pecan lovers were out of luck. Pleased with the generally enthusiastic reaction to his idea, particularly among Georgia artists, Harris decided not only to continue distributing prints of an original painting each year, but also to launch a company-sponsored competition among the artists of an eight-state Southeastern region. More than two hundred and fifty artists, amateurs and professionals alike, entered paintings in the 1955 competition. Professional jurors selected the best entries, which were exhibited by the Atlanta Art Association, and prizes were awarded to the three outstanding paintings. Mindful of his customers' taste in art, Harris prudently reserved the right to choose from among *all* the entries the one that would be reproduced as the "Painting of the Year." During the next two years, the competition grew in scope and stature as a ninth state was added and entries were systematically solicited through art magazines, art schools, museums, newspapers and mailing lists.

Harris had clearly started something, but in 1957 his company made a move which threw a cloud of uncertainty across the future of the competition. The Atlanta Paper Company merged with the much larger Mead Corporation, based in Dayton, Ohio. Harris became president of Mead's Packaging Division in Atlanta, as well as a vice president and director of the parent corporation. His art-support program came up only briefly during the merger negotiations, but the attitude of the rather conservative Dayton paper-makers was frankly skeptical. However, the "Painting of the Year" competition was continued as part of the packaging division's public-relations program.

The competition remained on this basis for the next few years, but it encountered growing opposition from a few Mead executives. Though "Painting of the Year" reproductions were made available at cost to other Mead divisions, which made increasing use of them as gifts, there were stubborn holdouts at headquarters who thought the program should be cancelled. The mixture of indifference and disapproval undoubtedly arises within any company that sponsors major art, cultural and public service projects. The candor of Mead on this point is unusual and refreshing.

On one occasion, Harris saved the project only by offering to assume sponsorship through his family's foundation, provided Mead would turn over the growing collection of 16 company-owned pictures, which he valued at $50,000. D. F. Morris, then Mead's president, was impressed. "If it's worth that much to you," he told Harris, "we'll keep it."

However, merely keeping the program alive represented a rather hollow victory. Much as he took pride in his inspiration, Harris realized the project was going nowhere unless sponsorship could somehow be lifted from the division to the corporate level.

This finally occurred in 1961 as an increasing number of Mead officers and employees came to realize the unique aspects of the project and its potential as a sales promotion aid. The adoption of the program as a corporate activity was marked by the establishment of a "Painting of the Year Committee," on which Harris sat as chairman with six other senior executives. The advocate now had just one vote, but he was delighted to cast it with the others for prompt expansion. In 1963, a second regional competition and exhibition was established, embracing eleven Midwestern states; the climax was a juried show in Chicago, which won Mead its first important attention in national art circles. Selections from the Southeastern and Midwestern shows were assembled for an exhibition which toured museums from coast to coast for sixteen months. Within a year of becoming a corporate program, the budget doubled, and then swiftly began to double again.

Those who had early doubts about the program's usefulness began to be converted after the Chicago show and the traveling exhibition revealed some of the unsuspected advantages of art-support. J. W. McSwiney, now Mead's executive vice president, discovered, for one thing, how art could facilitate "making contacts you couldn't make any other way." Customers and prospective customers invited to the black-tie openings literally saw Mead in a new light, and many of them came away impressed. No sales were made in the galleries, but Mead found that certain doors opened more easily later on.

Even as he talks about art being useful in a business way, however, McSwiney declines to follow that line of reasoning to a false conclusion. "I don't know that you can defend an art program in clear, concise business terms. There are too many intangibles. It's like our decision, many years ago, to open the company's timberlands to hunters and campers in spite of the fire hazard. In both cases, we're trying to answer an environmental need, and I think that's a good enough defense."

As the tenth anniversary of the Painting of the Year program approached, Mead began to lay ambitious plans for a truly national competition and exhibition. First, however, it sought frank, objective counsel from experts. A dozen former jurors came to the New York offices for a day-long discussion with a group of Mead representatives. This meeting reflected the company's increasing reliance on the distinguished curators and critics who served as jurors. The old system of awarding prizes had been abandoned in favor of one under which the jurors recommended certain paintings for acquisition for The Mead Collection and honored others by designating them "Paintings of Distinction." The "Painting of the Year" was selected from among those recommended for acquisition: first, the jurors ranked these paintings in order of preference, and then the members of the Mead committee followed a similar procedure; the painting which enjoyed the highest composite score was thus identified. Having brought the jurors into close cooperation with the program, Mead could turn to them confidently for candid criticism and advice.

A working memorandum prepared for the New York meeting posed this basic question: "How does Mead run a national or regional competition aimed at giving the greatest opportunity to a large number of artists without compromising the quality of the exhibition?" The former jurors pointed out that juried shows, such as Mead sponsored, were unattractive to established artists who had little or nothing to gain from entering competitions with unknowns. They also pointed out that Mead was simply not offering enough money to bring out paintings of first-rate quality.

After carefully studying these and other observations, Mead with the assistance of its public relations counsel, Ruder & Finn, Inc., evolved the plans for the nationwide program called Art Across America. In the first half of 1965, four regional competitions were held, under the co-sponsorship of Mead and leading museums in Boston, Atlanta, Columbus (Ohio) and San Francisco. In all, there were three thousand entries. From each regional competition, jurors selected works for exhibition at the sponsoring museum. The four resulting shows were judged by Peter Selz, of the Museum of Modern Art, who selected twenty-nine paintings which, with those invited, made up a fifty-work national exhibition that toured museums in sixteen cities during 1965 and 1966.

Mead introduced several innovations. Each of the three jurors in the four regions was permitted to invite two established artists to enter the regional show, with the assurance that these paintings would automatically qualify for showing in the national exhibition. This, it was decided, would tend to upgrade the overall quality of the exhibition. Mead also established a $25,000 purchase fund, a figure deemed large enough to attract artists already commanding a good price for their works under commission. Whether they were competitive or invited, the works were priced by the entrants at the outset of the program. Mead bought fifteen of the paintings. Those it did not buy were offered for sale in the regional shows and, if they qualified for the national exhibition, were offered throughout the tour.

Art Across America created a new vehicle for Mead's program

— the biannual, multi-regional competition and exhibition — and this sweeping departure, plus the $200,000 price-tag, to be spent over three years, required some strenuous salesmanship within the corporate committee. As Harris has publicly declared, "approval was by no means pre-assured or certain. We are a big company, with many executives who have different perspectives. These perspectives are certainly valuable in the operation of mills and converting plants and in marketing activities, but they do not simplify the matter of selling a concept, the value of which a number of our people were openly and honestly dubious about." But approval was won, and the results, after intensive planning and mastery of endless detail, more than satisfied the skeptics.

The results can be measured, by those who prefer tangibles, in the bales of magazine and newspaper clippings mentioning Mead favorably. They can be measured in the thick folders of congratulatory letters, including a handwritten note from artist Robert Harvey, whose "Brother Home on Leave" the company purchased and honored as the 1966 Painting of the Year ("I am immensely pleased...because of the highly professional way the exhibition was conducted and the regard The Mead Corporation seems to have for the artists. Some of the museums and galleries could learn from them...") And sales of Mead products could doubtless be traced to this exposure and the personal contacts the exhibition provided.

But the intangible, almost indefinable, results were no less impressive. Years of involvement on a limited scale, during which Mead had learned much, suddenly culminated in a well-executed ascent to the heights of corporate patronage. An executive who had harbored doubts remembers the opening of the national exhibition, a benefit for the American Association of Museums, at the elegant Knoedler Galleries on New York's Fifty-seventh Street. Amid the glittering throng of invited guests, he found himself next to Helen Hayes, the first lady of the American theater, and decided to ask why she had come. "I'm always telling people to support the arts, and that's what Mead is doing," she replied. "So I had to support *you*."

Among the famous and the obscure, Mead has made friends through its support of art. By its encouragement of new art, it has gained the respect and good will of uncounted artists. (A woman in Florida, who sold her first painting through a Mead-sponsored show, wrote to inform the company that she had used the $100 to buy two shares of Mead stock.) By identifying itself with artistic innovation, Mead has been able to draw closer to the cultural and intellectual leadership of many communities, and to make the point—which it feels strongly about—that profit-seeking corporate enterprise, itself engaged in innovation, makes such art support possible. Among young people, the sponsorship of contemporary, often experimental art hopefully will assist recruiting. The Mead Collection is touring colleges throughout the country.

Of course, not everyone is enthusiastic. Some Mead salesmen remain unconverted ("my six-year-old can paint better than *that*") and customers occasionally lose their tempers over Mead's sponsorship of "beatnik art." One letter from an irate businessman, prompted by the 1965 Painting of the Year, William C. Kortlander's "Participants," is still passed around in Dayton: "Our country, at present, is in enough turmoil and strife caused by rebellious 'participants'... [Mead should not be] publishing paintings condoning and encouraging this rebellious action... very poor taste... untimely... completely misrepresented the corporate image of Mead...."

In a way, this letter, which was answered with a strong defense of artistic freedom, is one of the proudest trophies in the extensive correspondence Mead has accumulated as the result of distributing more than one hundred thousand "Painting of the Year" reproductions. Beyond a doubt, the outraged gentleman responded to art—wrong-headedly, to be sure—and took seriously its relevance to contemporary American life. And this, after all, is what Mead is seeking.

In the Foreword to the catalogue of the Art Across America exhibition, President George H. Pringle reaffirmed what his company believes about the businessman and the artist:

"Businessmen and women today have a clearer appreciation of the role of the artist than ever before. This is not to say we completely understand or enjoy, or even approve, all they say and do. Nor is there any reason we should. What we have learned is that their works—those we enjoy and those we do not—can tell us much about the society in which we live and work. Those of us in The Mead Corporation need this kind of insight as much as anyone."

THE
MEAD
COLLECTION

1   Ida Kohlmeyer, *Fantasy No. 2*

2   Carroll Cloar, *The Red Haw Tree*

3　Frank A. Rampolla, *Self-Portrait*

4   Harrison Covington, *Man Against Landscape*

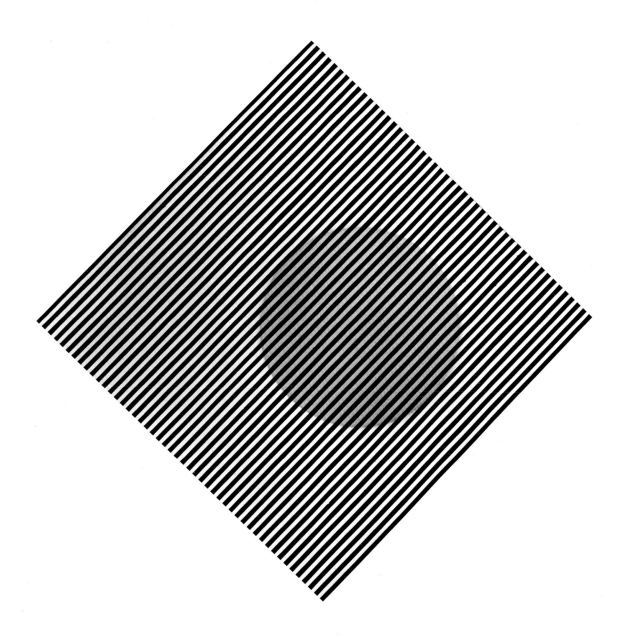

6   William Moreland, *Put Down Your Nets*

7   Carl Sublett, *Sea Wood*

8   Krimmer Brams, *The Prompter*

9   Tom Cavanaugh, *Nine Riders*

10   Robert H. Laessig, *Autumn Mist*

11   James Yarbrough, *Noreen and Laurie*

12 Fred Messersmith, *Shore Birds*

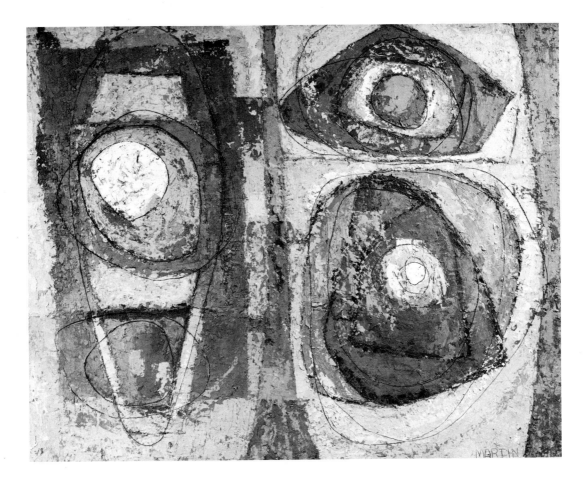

13   Walt Martin, *Untitled No. 8*

14 Syd Solomon, *Sunken Ship*

15   William C. Kortlander, *Participants*

16   Edward Ruschá, *Flash, L. A. Times,*

17   Donald Roberts, *Mutuality—April 1961*

18 Keith Boyle, *Flyin' Home*

19 Joseph S. Perrin, *Still Life with Blue Vase*   65

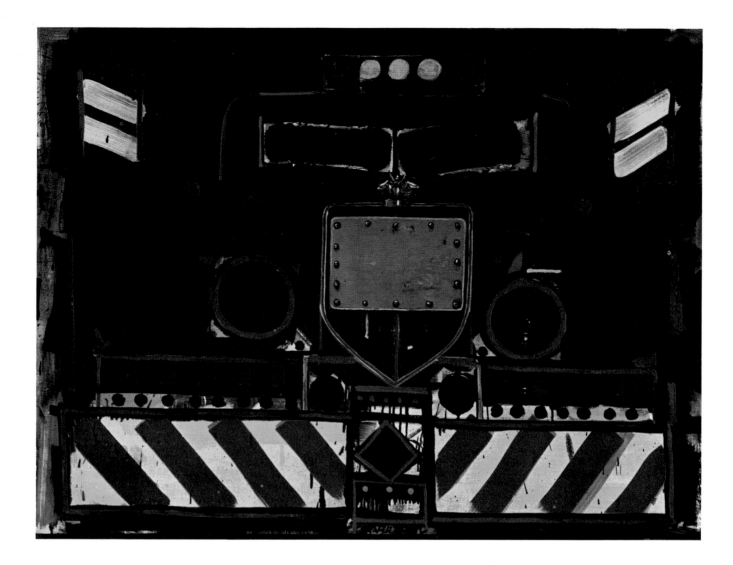

20 Maurice Brown, *Night Truck*

21   Tony Scornavacca, *Still Life with Chairs*

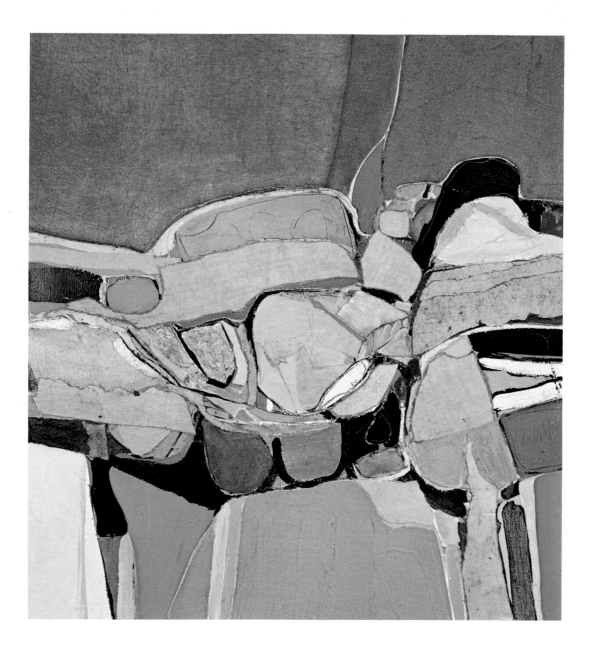

22   James E. Grant, *Standing Collage*

24 Ben Shute, *Headland Maine*

26 Joseph Cox, *Men and Nets*

27   Claire Salzberg, *No Title*

28 George Beattie, *Georgia Nocturne*

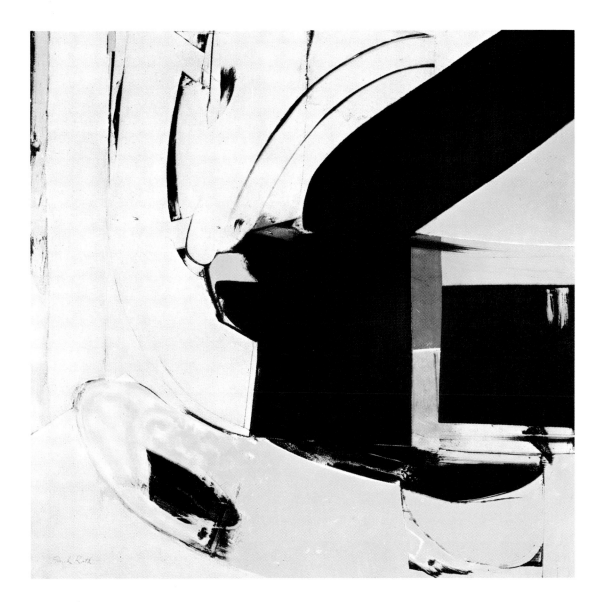

30 Herman Maril, *Sand and Water*

31 William Pachner, *Night Event*

32 Hugh Townley, *Next Wednesday*

33 Ida Kohlmeyer, *Radiance*

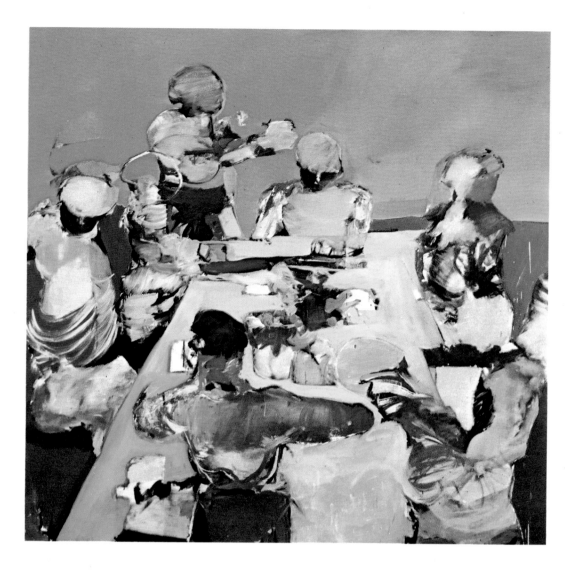

34   Judy Lodge, *The Table*

35 Paul Jenkins, *Phenomena with Veils*

36 Syd Solomon, *Summer Storm*

38   James Yarbrough, *Country Store*

39 Robert L. Hartman, *Scrapbook for an Early Birdman*

40   Paul Horiuchi, *Canyon of Commerce*

41   Robert Gelinas, *New Spring*

42   Fred Attyah, *Tree Forms*

43　Robert Harvey, *Brother Home on Leave*

44 Edward Ross, *Facade,*

LIST OF ILLUSTRATIONS—THE MEAD COLLECTION

23   James F. Gill, *The Executive Triptych*, 1964, crayon/paper/board, 36 x 75.

24   Ben Shute, *Headland Maine*, watercolor/paper, 21 x 29.

25   Howard Thomas, *Festival 41*, oil/board, 48 x 30.

26   Joseph Cox, *Men and Nets*, tempera/board, 23½ x 39½. 1955 Mead Painting of the Year.

27   Claire Salzberg, *No Title*, oil, 51 x 49.

28   George Beattie, *Georgia Nocturne*, egg tempera/board, 25 x 29½. 1954 Mead Painting of the Year.

29   Frank Roth, *Lady McGowan's Dream*, 1964, oil/canvas, 60 x 68.

30   Herman Maril, *Sand and Water*, oil/canvas, 37 x 49. 1963 Mead Painting of the Year.

31   William Pachner, *Night Even*, oil/board, 46½ x 46½.

32   Hugh Townley, *Next Wednesday*, 1963, various woods, 33½ x 74.

33   Ida Kohlmeyer: *Radiance*, oil/canvas, 50 x 49.

34   Judy Lodge, *The Table*, 1965, oil/canvas, 70 x 72.

35   Paul Jenkins, *Phenomena with Veils*, 1965, oil/canvas, 60 x 40.

36   Syd Solomon, *Summer Storm*, oil/canvas, 39 x 37.

37   George Beattie, *Italian Nocturne*, polymer tempera/canvas, 47 x 61¼.

38   James Yarbrough, *Country Store*, oil/canvas, 54 x 55. 1962 Mead Painting of the Year.

39   Robert L. Hartman, *Scrapbook for an Early Birdman*, 1965, acrylic collage, 50 x 45.

40   Paul Horiuchi, *Canyon of Commerce*, 1965, casein collage, 71 x 61.

41   Robert Gelinas, *New Spring*, oil/collage, 53½ x 59.

42   Fred Attyah, *Tree Forms*, watercolor/paper, 50 x 41.

43   Robert Harvey, *Brother Home on Leave*, 1964, oil/canvas, 60 x 52. 1966 Mead Painting of the Year.

44   Edward Ross, *Facade*, oil/canvas, 37 x 50.

Illustrations and jacket printed on 100-pound Mead Superb Enamel, glossy finish paper
Text printed on 70-pound Mead Suede-Wove finish paper
Composition by Progressive Typography, Inc.
Typeface, Bodoni Book with Italics, assorted sizes
Color lithography and jacket by Barnes Press, Inc.
Text lithography by Panarama Press, Inc.
Binding by American Book-Stratford Press, Inc.
Design by Chermayeff & Geismar